FIVE LATE
STRING QUARTETS

Antonín Dvořák

DOVER PUBLICATIONS, INC.

NEW YORK

Bibliographical Note

This Dover edition, first published in 1986 and reprinted in 2011, is an unabridged republication of five separate quartet volumes (*Quartett für 2 Violinen, Bratsche und Violoncell;* Op. 51, 1879; Op. 61, 1882; Op. 96, 1894; Op. 106, 1896; Op. 105, 1896) as published by N. Simrock, Berlin.

The publisher is grateful to The George Sherman Dickinson Music Library, Vassar College, for lending its copies of the five quartets for photographing.

International Standard Book Number

ISBN-13: 978-0-486-25135-6
ISBN-10: 0-486-25135-7

Manufactured in the United States by LSC Communications
4500053580
www.doverpublications.com

CONTENTS

Quartet No. 10 in E-Flat Major, Op. 51

DUMKA.
(Elegie.)

Andante con moto. M.M. ♩ = 63.

Vivace. ♩.= 86.

Poco meno mosso.

Poco più mosso.

Andante con moto.

24   Quartet No. 10 in E-Flat Major

ROMANZE.

Andante con moto. M.M. ♪ = 100.

FINALE.

Allegro assai. M.M. ♩= 126.

Poco meno mosso.

Tempo I.

Poco meno mosso.

Tempo I.

Poco meno mosso.

Più Allegro.

Quartet No. 11 in C Major, Op. 61

I.

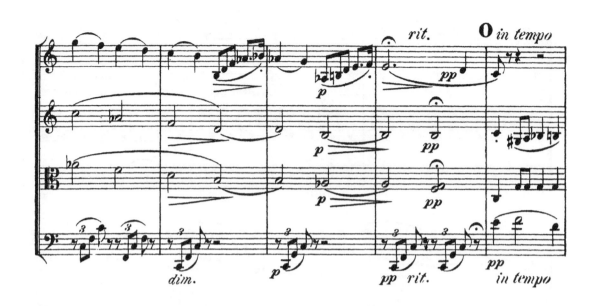

II.

Poco Adagio e molto cantabile.

III.
SCHERZO.

Allegro vivo.

Trio.
L'istesso tempo.

Scherzo D. C. al Fine.

IV.

FINALE.

Vivace.

Quartet No. 12 in F Major, Op. 96
("The American")

I.

II.

III.

Molto vivace. M.M. ♩. = 72.

molto rit. in tempo

Finale.

Quartet No. 13 in G Major, Op. 106

I.

166   Quartet No. 13 in G Major

II.

Poco a poco animato.

Poco a poco animato.

molto appassionato

Tempo I.($\flat$ = 63.)

III.

Molto vivace. M. M. ♩ = 92.

6 Un poco meno mosso.

Tempo I. ($\left.\text{♩.} = 92.\right)$

Finale.
IV.
Andante sostenuto. M.M. ♩=58.

Allegro con fuoco. M.M. ♩=138.

7 Allegro con fuoco. Tempo I. M.M. ♩ = 138.

Quartet No. 14 in A-Flat Major, Op. 105
I.

II.

Molto vivace (M. M. $\circ$. = 92)

Da Capo dal Segno ℀ sin' al Fine.

III.

Lento e molto cantabile. M.M. ♪ = 116.

IV.